What's in this book

This book belongs to

T0351522

_____

请喝茶 At the Chinese restaurant

学习内容 Contents

沟通 Communication

称呼家庭成员
Address family members

请他人喝饮料
Offer someone a drink

表达疑问
Express doubt

生词 New words

⭐ 我们　　　　we, us

⭐ 你们　　　　you

⭐ 他们／她们　they, them

⭐ 爷爷　　　　grandfather, grandpa

⭐ 奶奶　　　　grandmother, grandma

⭐ 请　　　　　please

⭐ 个　　　　　(measure word)

⭐ 呢　　　　　(interrogative particle)

背景介绍：
周末上午，浩浩一家和爷爷奶奶一起去中国酒家饮茶。

浩浩爷爷

浩浩奶奶

茶　　　　tea

说话　　　to speak

办法　　　idea, method

句式 Sentence patterns

爷爷奶奶，请喝茶。
Grandma and Grandpa,
please have some tea.

怎么办呢？
What should I do?

文化 Cultures

中国孝的概念
Filial piety in Chinese culture

跨学科学习 Project

制作糖果相框，写中文节日卡
Make a photo frame using sweets
and write a card in Chinese

参考答案：
1　Yes, I do. I like Chinese food./No, I don't. I am not fond of Chinese food.
2　I like going with my family/friends/schoolmates.
3　We usually talk over meals./We sometimes watch TV when having meals.

Get ready

1 Do you like going to Chinese restaurants?

2 Who do you like going with?

3 What do you do when you have meals with your family?

读一读 Read

故事大意：
周末上午，浩浩一家和爷爷奶奶一起去中国酒家饮茶。大家只做自己的事，互不交流，令奶奶很失望。最后浩浩和奶奶想了个办法，打破僵局，制造欢乐的家庭聚餐气氛。

wǒ men
我们

"我们"指包括自己（说话人）在内，两个或两个以上人物的称呼。

星期日，我们和爷爷奶奶一起上茶楼。

参考问题和答案：
Who does 我们 refer to? (It refers to Hao Hao, Ling Ling and their parents.)

4

yé ye
爷爷

爸爸的爸爸我们叫"爷爷"。

tā men
他们

"他们"指除了自己（说话人）和对方（听话人）以外，两个或两个以上人物的称呼。"他们"可指全属男性或男女并存。

爸爸和爷爷看球，他们不说话。

参考问题和答案：

1 What are Dad and Grandpa doing? (They are watching sports on the tablet.)

2 Are they talking to each other? (No, they are not.)

"她们"指除了自己（说话人）和对方（听话人）以外，两个或两个以上女性的称呼。

tā men
她们

妈妈看手机、姐姐画画，她们不说话。

参考问题和答案：

1 What are Ling Ling and Mum doing? (Ling Ling is drawing, and Mum is on her phone.)

2 Are they talking to each other? (No, they are not.)

nǎi nai
奶奶

没有人说话，也没有人喝茶。奶奶不高兴。

参考问题和答案：
How does Grandma feel? Why? (She feels upset because nobody is talking to each other or drinking tea.)

"呢"用在句末，表示疑问
语气。如"怎么办呢？"

怎么办呢？我有一个办法。

参考问题和答案：

1 What is Hao Hao planning to do? (He is planning to do something to improve the situation.)
2 What do Hao Hao and Grandma do? (Hao Hao shuts Dad's tablet and Grandma takes off
   Grandpa's glasses.)

"你们"指除了自己（说话人），包括对方（听话人）在内，两个或两个以上人物的称呼。

nǐ men
你们

qǐng
请

hē chá
喝茶

"请"用于希望对方做某事时，表示礼貌。此处是晚辈对长辈的礼貌和尊敬。

参考问题和答案：

1 What are Hao Hao and Ling Ling doing? (They are serving tea to their grandparents.)
2 Do you think everyone is happier now than before? Why? (Everyone is happier now because they are talking to each other.)

"爷爷奶奶，你们请喝茶。"我和姐姐说。

Let's think

提醒学生回忆故事，观察第5至7页。

1 **Why is Grandma unhappy? Tick the boxes.**

2 **Look carefully. Circle the Chinese food.**

提醒学生有些食物是在故事中出现过的。可说说中国特色食物有饺子和包子等，也可让学生基于自己已知的西方食物，做排除法。

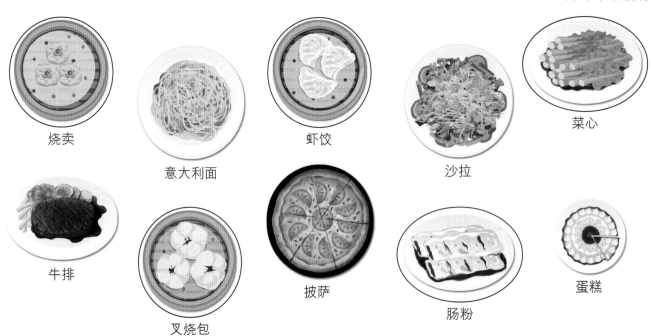

烧卖　意大利面　虾饺　沙拉　菜心

牛排　叉烧包　披萨　肠粉　蛋糕

10

New words

延伸活动：
1 老师可以指着图片上浩浩的爸爸、妈妈、爷爷、奶奶和姐姐，让学生说出相应的亲属称谓。
2 老师用手势表示群体"你们""我们""他们""她们"，由学生说出相应的人称代词。

1 Learn the new words.

2 Complete the sentences. Write the letters.

提醒学生注意箭头指向的说话人。
1 别人　2 伊森　3 浩浩　4 浩浩

a 我们　　b 你们　　c 他们　　d 她们　　e 爷爷　　f 奶奶

1 _d_ 喜欢唱歌。

2 _a_ 有一个足球。

3 _c_ 是我的 _e_ 和 _f_ 。

4 _b_ 请喝茶。

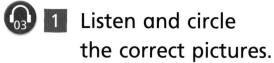
听听说说 Listen and say

第一题录音稿：
1 奶奶喜欢红色的苹果。
2 爷爷星期三看书，星期六画画。
3 那不是我们的本子，那是他们的。

🎧 03 **1** Listen and circle the correct pictures.

🎧 04 **2** Look at the pictures. Listen to the stor

1

2

3

① 爷爷奶奶，请喝茶。

③ 我有一个苹果。

我有两个苹果。

第二题参考问题和答案：

1　How do you say "Grandpa and Grandma, please have some tea." in Chinese? (爷爷奶奶，请喝茶。)

2　Do you show respect for your elders at home? (Yes, I always offer food to my elders first.)

...d say.

 3 Listen and read. Role-play with your friends.

1

2

"吗"和"呢"都用于句末表疑问。"吗"字句一般用"是"或"不是"等是非词回答；"呢"字句则需根据问题用具体答案回答。

13

Task

Stick a picture of your grandparents in the space below. Tell your friends about them.

提醒学生带与爷爷奶奶的照片回学校，并贴在空白处。若空间不够，可钉在本页左上角。

我的爷爷奶奶叫……

Paste your photo here.

我们一起玩。

我们一起画画。

Game

游戏方法：
学生两人一组，一人指着书上的活动询问，另一人回答。可角色互换，对话形式活泼开放。
对话句式参考："你（不）喜欢……吗？""我（不）喜欢……""我（不）喜欢……，你呢？"

Point to the shapes and find out what your friend likes or does not like to do.

你喜欢踢足球吗？

喝茶

我喜欢踢足球。

踢足球

我喜欢唱歌，你呢？

和小狗玩

画画

吃水果

看书

我不喜欢唱歌，我喜欢和小狗玩。

唱歌

Song

Listen and sing.

"请"字表示礼貌，多用于下级对上级，晚辈对长辈。

爷爷奶奶，你们请喝茶。

爸爸妈妈，你们请吃水果。

哥哥姐姐，你们喝果汁吗？

弟弟妹妹，

你们和我一起玩吗？

课堂用语 Classroom language

玩游戏。

Play a game.

赢了。输了。

I won. I lost.

写一写 Write

1 Learn and trace the stroke. "竖弯钩"即先竖，再弯，最后钩。从上到下，从左到右书写，笔画之间没有间断。

竖弯钩

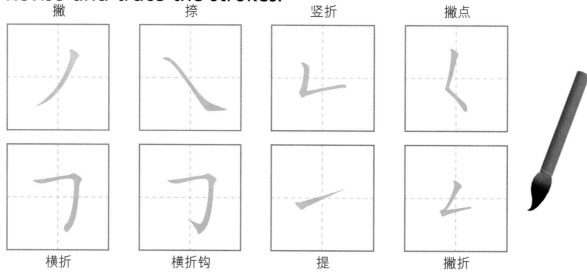

提醒学生先回忆笔画形态及其写法，再进行描写。

2 Revise and trace the strokes.

撇	捺	竖折	撇点

横折	横折钩	提	撇折

3 There are six components in the picture. Can you write them?

提醒学生仔细看图，注意区分男人和女人。

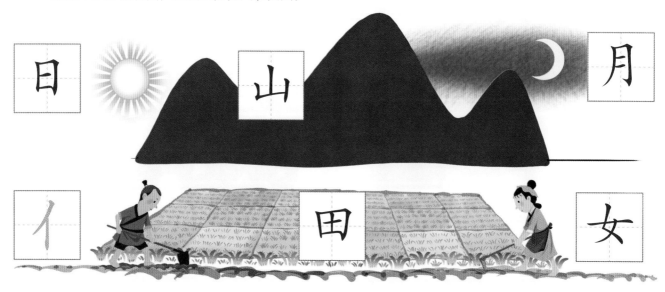

日　山　月
亻　田　女

4 Trace and write the characters.

提醒学生，用单人旁表示男性，女字旁表示女性，从而区分"他"与"她"的用法，并让学生注意这两个字左侧部件写小一些，右侧写大一些。

5 Write and say.

学生完成填空后，教师根据图片总结："他们"指全部男性或男女并存的若干人；"她们"则特指若干女性。

汉字小常识 *Did you know?*

When talking about more than one person, remember to use 们 .

Read the words aloud.

左侧的词汇都表示一个人，右侧词汇是在后面加了"们"来表示两个或两个以上的人。

你
他
她
男孩
女孩
朋友

我

我们

你们
他们
她们
男孩们
女孩们
朋友们

延伸活动：学生两人一组，一人说出单数人称，另一人说出相应的复数人称。反之亦可练习。

多元学习 Connections

Cultures

1 Do you know how Chinese people show respect for their elders?

"孝"是中华文化中极为重要的观念，指晚辈应该尊重和回报长辈。

孝

Filial piety means to be good to one's parents and the elders. It is very important in Chinese culture.

陪长辈散步

多陪伴长辈

与长辈分享

关心长辈的日常生活和健康

2 How do you show respect for your elders? Write on the note paper.

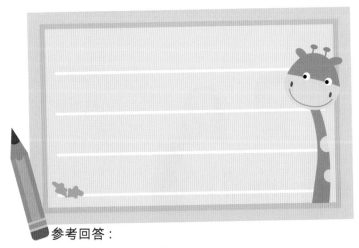

参考回答：

1 I visit my grandparents every Saturday. We usually go for a walk and then watch a film at home.

2 I help my grandparents with chores.

Project

材料：两张不同颜色的卡纸、一把剪刀、一瓶胶水、一瓶彩色糖果。

1 Would you like to give your parents a special photo frame? Follow the steps to make one.

分别将两张卡纸剪成一大一小的长方形框。

最后将照片从正前方放入做好的相框中。

先用胶水涂满小长方形框四边的外侧（内侧不用涂胶水，用来放进并卡住照片），贴到大长方形框正上方。再用糖果贴满相框四周。

2 Make your grandparents a card. Draw their faces and colour the Chinese words.

提醒学生画自己和爷爷奶奶的脸，并将气球中的汉字上色。可以将完成的卡片带回家，展示给爷爷奶奶看，并将卡片里的中文说给他们听。

游戏方法：
学生从上往下依次完成每个幸运饼干所在的小任务。

1 Read the messages in the fortune cookies. Answer the questions and do the tasks.

我喜欢学中文

How do we say 'we' and 'you' in Chinese?

我们；你们

👄 爸爸妈妈，请喝茶。

她是谁？ Answer in Chinese.

她是浩浩的奶奶。

他是谁？ Answer in Chinese.

他是浩浩的爷爷。

Write 'he' and 'she' in Chinese.

他　她

👄 星期六，他们看书，你呢？

👄 我喜欢喝水，不喜欢喝果汁。

Does your friend like tea? Ask him/her in Chinese.

你喜欢喝茶吗？

2 Work with your friend. Colour the stars and the chilies.

Words	说	读	写
我们	☆	☆	🌶
你们	☆	☆	🌶
他们	☆	☆	🌶
她们	☆	☆	🌶
爷爷	☆	☆	🌶
奶奶	☆	☆	🌶
请	☆	☆	🌶
个	☆	☆	🌶
呢	☆	☆	🌶

Words and sentences	说	读	写
茶	☆	🌶	🌶
说话	☆	🌶	🌶
办法	☆	🌶	🌶
爷爷奶奶，请喝茶。	☆	🌶	🌶
怎么办呢？	☆	🌶	🌶

Address family members	☆
Offer someone a drink	☆
Express doubt	☆

3 What does your teacher say?

评核建议：

根据学生课堂表现，分别给予"太棒了！(Excellent!)"、"不错！(Good!)"或"继续努力！(Work harder!)"的评价，再让学生圈出上方对应的表情，以记录自己的学习情况。

My teacher says ...

分享 Sharing

延伸活动：
1 学生用手遮盖英文，读中文单词，并思考单词意思；
2 学生用手遮盖中文单词，看着英文说出对应的中文单词；
3 学生三人一组，尽量运用中文单词分角色复述故事。

Words I remember

我们	wǒ men	we, us
你们	nǐ men	you
他们／她们	tā men/ tā men	they, them
爷爷	yé ye	grandfather, grandpa
奶奶	nǎi nai	grandmother, grandma
请	qǐng	please
个	gè	(measure wor
呢	ne	(interrogative particle)

茶	chá	tea
说话	shuō huà	to speak
办法	bàn fǎ	idea, method

Other words

上	shàng	to go to
茶楼	chá lóu	Chinese restaurant
手机	shǒu jī	cell phone
也	yě	also, too
高兴	gāo xìng	glad, happy

OXFORD

UNIVERSITY PRESS

Oxford University Press is a department of the University of Oxford.
It furthers the University's objective of excellence in research, scholarship,
and education by publishing worldwide. Oxford is a registered trade mark of
Oxford University Press in the UK and in certain other countries

Published in Hong Kong by
Oxford University Press (China) Limited
39th Floor, One Kowloon, 1 Wang Yuen Street, Kowloon Bay,
Hong Kong

© Oxford University Press (China) Limited 2017

The moral rights of the author have been asserted

First Edition published in 2017

All rights reserved. No part of this publication may be reproduced, stored in a
retrieval system, or transmitted, in any form or by any means, without the prior
permission in writing of Oxford University Press (China) Limited, or as expressly
permitted by law, by licence, or under terms agreed with the appropriate
reprographics rights organization. Enquiries concerning reproduction outside
the scope of the above should be sent to the Rights Department, Oxford
University Press (China) Limited, at the address above

You must not circulate this work in any other form
and you must impose this same condition on any acquirer

Illustrated by Anne Lee and Wildman

Photographs for reproduction permitted by Dreamstime.com

China National Publications Import & Export (Group) Corporation is an authorized distributor of
Oxford Elementary Chinese.

Please contact content@cnpiec.com.cn or 86-10-65856782

ISBN: 978-0-19-942981-3

10 9 8 7 6 5 4 3 2

Teacher's Edition
ISBN: 978-0-19-082203-3

10 9 8 7 6 5 4 3 2